Animals That Hibernate

Animals That Hibernate

Phyllis J. Perry

 LIBRARY

Franklin Watts
A Division of Scholastic Inc.
New York • Toronto • London • Auckland • Sydney
Mexico City • New Delhi • Hong Kong
Danbury, Connecticut

For Janet and Jill, who are much too busy to ever hibernate!

Note to readers: Definitions for words in **bold** can be found in the Glossary at the back of this book.

Photographs ©: Animals Animals: 46 (Bruce Davidson), cover (Breck P. Kent), 36 (Joe McDonald), 23 (Marty Stouffer); Liaison Agency, Inc./Daniel J. Cox: 16; Peter Arnold Inc./Lynn Rogers: 20, 21, 50; Photo Researchers, NY: 38, 39 (John M. Burnley), 15 (Jim W. Grace), 40, 41 (Jeff Lepore), 47 (Karl Maslowski), 5 left, 30, 31 (Tom McHugh), 49 (Tom McHugh/Steinhart Aquarium), 27 (John Mitchell), 53 (NASA/SPL), 28 (Stephen P. Parker), 32, 33 (Gary Retherford), 13 (Gregory K. Scott), 6, 34 (John Serrao), 2 (Merlin D. Tuttle/Bat Conservation Intl.); Visuals Unlimited: 44 (Bill Beatty), 10 (C. P. George), 9 (John Gerlach), 5 right, 18 (William Grenfell), 25 (Joe McDonald), 43 (Richard Thom), 52 (William J. Weber).

The cover image shows a hibernating eastern chipmunk. The image opposite the title page shows a cluster of hibernating bats.

Library of Congress Cataloging-in-Publication Data

Perry, Phyllis Jean.
 Animals that hibernate / by Phyllis J. Perry
   p. cm.— (Watts Library)
 Includes bibliographical references and index (p.).
 ISBN 0-531-11864-9 (lib. bdg.) 0-531-16572-8 (pbk.)
 1. Hibernation—Juvenile literature. [1. Hibernation. 2. Animals—Wintering.] I. Title. II. Series.

QL755 .P47 2001
591.56'5—dc21

00-043511

© 2001 Franklin Watts, a Division of Scholastic, Inc.
All rights reserved. Published simultaneously in Canada.
Printed in the United States of America.
 2 3 4 5 6 7 8 9 10 R 10 09 08 07 06 05 04 03 02

Contents

During the colder months, many animals disappear into winter homes like this black bear den.

Chapter One

When the Cold Comes

As winter approaches, gold and fiery orange leaves fall from quaking aspen and blanket the forest floor. Black bears that bumbled through the forest eating berries are gone. The yellow-bellied marmots that scurried among the rocks during the warmer months are nowhere to be seen. Since winter is on its way, many animals have already dug a deep burrow and are sleeping underground. It will be March or April before they emerge to bask in the warm sun again.

Wild animals survive winter in different ways. A variety of animals, such as hummingbirds and gray whales, **adapt** to the changing season by traveling or **migrating** to different areas in search of food. Other animals, such as gray squirrels and elk, add layers of fat and grow a thick fur coat to protect themselves during the cold season. Animals like the black bears and yellow-bellied marmots prepare a safe place to go to sleep until the weather turns warm and plants start growing again. This long sleep is called **hibernation**.

During hibernation, the animal's temperature drops, and its breathing and heart rate slow. This sluggish state is referred to as **torpor**. Torpor is different from regular nightly sleep, which lasts only a few hours. In hibernation, animals can sleep for months at a time.

Many different types of animals hibernate. Their bodies prepare for this change in different ways. In the fall, many warm-blooded animals begin eating large amounts of food that is stored as body fat. Yellow-bellied marmots, for example, are so fat at the end of summer that they waddle. But, while they are hibernating, nearly all the energy in their fat cells is turned into heat. This heat energy is used to keep them alive through their winter sleep.

During hibernation, some animals are "deep sleepers" while others are "light sleepers." A deep sleeper, like a woodchuck, is almost impossible to wake up during hibernation, while light sleepers, like bears, can be awakened easily. In a deep sleep, there is a large decrease in the animal's heartbeat, breathing rate, and body temperature. The animal's **metabolism** is reduced by thirty to one hundred times. A light sleeper undergoes bodily changes, too, but they are not as drastic. These changes in breathing and heart rate help conserve the animal's energy. A hibernating animal uses only enough energy to keep its body alive. When the animal uses all its stored energy, it wakes up in spring when food is available.

Some **cold-blooded** animals also hibernate. **Amphibians** find a protected spot and become inactive. Many fish become **torpid**, resting at the bottom of a lake or river. Some insects prepare for winter by becoming somewhat dehydrated and finding protected spots where they can survive.

The places where animals hibernate can vary as much as the depth and length of their sleep. Many animals stay snug in the ground in burrows and dens. Some animals huddle under dirt, leaves, logs, and stones, while others are hidden away in caves, crevices, or deep in the mud.

Some cold-blooded animals, like frogs, hibernate by burrowing deep into mud.

An arctic ground squirrel hibernates in a burrow.

Chapter Two

In Burrows

When it is time to hibernate, some animals make nests underground in burrows. Each animal's burrow can be different. Some burrows contain food storage chambers and there may be special rooms that the animals use as toilet areas. Animals can dig their own burrows or use abandoned burrows.

The depth of the burrow depends on the animal using it and the climate of the area. Many are between 5 and 10 feet (1.5 and 3 meters) deep, but where it is extremely cold an animal may dig its burrow as much as 30 feet (9.1 m) deep in order to survive. When the hibernator is ready to sleep, it plugs the entrance to the burrow using dirt, stones, or plant material. This keeps out the cold as well as unwanted visitors.

Ground Squirrel

There are more than two dozen species of ground squirrels in North America. Not all of them hibernate. Those that do make a nest of leaves and grasses in a burrow. The ground squirrel curls up into a snug ball and places its tail over its head. It is dark in the burrow and the only sound within is slow breathing.

The ground squirrel falls into a deep sleep that may last from 6 to 9 months. Gradually its heart rate and breathing slow, and its temperature drops from 90 degrees Fahrenheit to 40 degrees Fahrenheit (32.2 degrees Celsius to 4.4 degrees Celsius). During the long, cold winter, the ground squirrel wakes up every 3 or 4 weeks, eats some of its stored food, and then goes back to sleep again. The thirteen-lined ground squirrel awakes from hibernation shivering. The small muscles near the outside of its body squeeze and relax, over and over, making heat but also resulting in weight loss. In spring, it revives completely and goes in search of food and a mate.

Woodchuck

The woodchuck, with its coarse, grizzled brown fur, is one of the animals that hibernates in a burrow. It is also known as a groundhog or whistle pig. In late summer and early fall, the

groundhog starts eating more flowers, leaves, wild plant stems, and grains to store up extra fat for the winter. As the days shorten, a woodchuck digs a burrow with an entrance that slopes down to a depth of 5 feet (1.5 m) and runs about 40 feet (12 m) in length. It makes a nest lined with leaves and grasses in the burrow. Its burrow has several chambers and passageways that have different uses. One of the chambers is used as a bathroom. The woodchuck sleeps in the biggest chamber that is closest to the surface.

A woodchuck emerges from its burrow.

In September or October, the woodchuck stops eating and seals off its burrow with packed soil. The woodchuck rolls into a ball and falls asleep. Its breathing slows from 25 breaths a minute to 1 breath every 5 minutes. The heartbeat slows from 80 beats to only 4 beats a minute. Its temperature drops from 98°F (36.7°C) to only 37°F (2.7°C). During its 6-month winter nap, the woodchuck may wake up now and then to eat some stored food and use the toilet chamber. Then it goes back to its nest and sleeps again.

The woodchuck awakes in spring, weighing less than it did when it began its winter nap. Emerging from its burrow, the woodchuck is ready to eat and mate. During April and May, a female woodchuck has a **litter** of four or five pups. The adults and young will fatten during the summer months to be ready for the seasonal cycle of hibernation again.

Jumping Mouse

The jumping mouse is one of the smallest of all the hibernating **mammals**. It measures only 3 inches (7.5 centimeters) in length and weighs less than an ounce. As fall approaches, the jumping mouse puts on weight by eating seeds, beetles, spiders, and even decaying meat and fish. Before hibernating, the jumping mouse digs a special hibernating tunnel well below the **frost line**. It builds a nest at the end of the tunnel and lines it with grasses.

Sometime in September or October, a jumping mouse plugs the hole to its burrow and goes into its hibernating

chamber. It curls into a tight ball, wrapping its long tail around its body, and sleeps for as long as 7 months. As it sleeps, the jumping mouse's body temperature, breathing, and heart rate decrease. The jumping mouse will wake up occasionally to urinate.

When the jumping mouse comes out of hibernation in April or May, it hunts for food and a mate. Eighteen days after

The jumping mouse digs a burrow that reaches down below the frost line.

15

mating, female jumping mice have litters of four to six mice. The naked and helpless newborns weigh less than a gram each. The mother nurses the young and in only 6 weeks they are full-grown.

Eastern Chipmunk

The eastern chipmunk also spends the winter in hibernation. It has brown fur with black back stripes. When the chipmunk stuffs seeds in its cheek pouches during spring and summer, it looks as if it has mumps! The chipmunk stores the seeds and acorns underground during October and early November.

In the Fall, chipmunks store seeds and acorns underground.

When winter comes, the chipmunk plugs up the entrance of the burrow and sleeps in a room lined with dried leaves and grasses. The eastern chipmunk will wake often to nibble stored food. If it is warm enough, the chipmunk will go outside for brief periods.

In February or March, eastern chipmunks become active again. They hunt for food and they mate. A month after mating, the females have litters of onc to nine babies. The mother nurses her babies until they are about 3 months old. Then they are ready to go out and hunt for food.

When they are old enough, the young dig their own burrows under roots or rocks or even under a cabin. Their tunnels twist and turn and are only about 2 inches (5 cm) wide, but may continue for 30 feet (9.1 m). Tunnels are dug below the freezing line, usually about 5 feet (1.5 m) deep.

Black bears
hibernate in dens
when the weather
turns cold.

Chapter Three

In Dens

Animals like bears, skunks, and raccoons look for dens to sleep in when the weather turns cold. Dens can take many forms, but they must be spots where the hibernating animal can feel secure and reasonably hope it will not be disturbed. Sometimes dens are shallow caves or spaces in a rock pile. A den could be a dirt room among the roots of a living tree, an old hollow log on a forest floor, or an upright dead tree trunk.

The black bear is the most common bear in North America. Its thick fur coat may be brown, black, gray, or cinnamon-colored. Black bears spend between

4 and 7 months hibernating in winter dens. Many scientists call the black bear's winter sleep hibernation. Other scientists do not think black bears are true hibernators because the bears are light sleepers. They can wake up and wander around on warmer winter days. Also, a bear's body temperature does not drop as much as other animals during hibernation.

Before winter arrives, the bears have grown fat from eating berries, fruit, nuts, mice, insects, and honey. The stored fat will allow the bear to survive through the winter when food is scarce. As the colder weather approaches, it is harder for the bear to find food. The bear then finds a cave or digs a den where it can hibernate. The temperature of a hibernating bear drops about 5 to 10 degrees. Its heart rate slows from 60 to 90 beats a minute to only 8 to 40 beats a minute.

While in her winter den, a mother black bear, or sow, will give birth to one to three cubs. She nurses and cares for the young, which are about 8 inches

This mother bear emerges from her den with her three cubs.

(20 cm) long and weigh about 0.5 pounds (0.23 kilograms). In the spring, the mother and young leave the den in search of food and drink. Throughout the spring, summer, and fall, the mother bear teaches the cubs how to find food. The following winter, the sow and her cubs usually hibernate together.

Grizzly Bear

Grizzlies are members of the brown bear family who get their name because their outer fur, whether blond or dark brown, is frosted or grizzled with gray. A male grizzly bear is very strong and weighs between 300 and 1,700 pounds (136 and 770 kg). Grizzlies have long claws, keen hearing, and a sharp sense of smell.

Grizzly bears eat both plants and animals, including wild fruits, nuts, roots of plants, insects, and animal carcasses. Before winter sets in, grizzly bears eat a large amount of food that they store as fat to last them through their hibernation. When they are ready to hibernate, grizzly bears use their sharp claws to dig a chamber about 6 feet (1.8 m) across in a location where deep snow will cover the entrance. Grizzlies line their beds with moss, grass, or the branches of fir trees.

Polar Sleep

The polar bear is the largest of all the bears. Polar bears eat seals, walruses, mosses, and lichens. Only the female polar bear hibernates. When the female is pregnant or has young cubs, she leaves the ice and water to go inland where she dens up for the winter.

This grizzly bear is preparing for hibernation inside a den.

They begin hibernating between the months of October and December. Once grizzly bears enter their dens, their heart rates slow from their usual 40 or 50 beats a minute to 10 or 12 beats a minute. Their temperature drops just a few degrees, and their breathing slows. Grizzly bears are light sleepers, so they may wake up if they are disturbed. Grizzly bears hibernate for 5 to 6 months. Male grizzly bears usually leave their winter dens between March and April.

During January or February, while still in a drowsy state in their dens, female grizzlies have one to four cubs, with two being average. Each cub weighs only about 1 pound (0.5 kg) and measures about 9 inches long (23 cm). The cubs are blind and helpless at birth and nurse from their mother until it is time to leave the den. When the cubs emerge from the den with their mother between April and May, they weigh about 20 pounds (9.1 kg).

Striped Skunk

Another light sleeper is the striped skunk. It is about the size of a house cat with a small head, short legs, and a long, bushy tail. Most of its fur is black but there is a white stripe down its face, white on the back of its head, and two white stripes along its back. Skunks eat berries, insects, mice, moles, shrews, or rats.

When the temperature drops, the striped skunk goes to its winter den in a hollow tree or log, or even in an empty burrow dug by a woodchuck. In cold areas, it may dig its den below the frost line at a depth of 6 to 12 feet (1.8 to 3.6 m).

Snug Comfort

The striped skunk's nest is lined with as much as a bushel basket (35 liters) of dried leaves and grass.

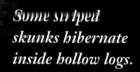

Some striped skunks hibernate inside hollow logs.

Several striped skunks may huddle together in one nest. The skunk's temperature drops slightly during hibernation and its breathing slows. But it awakens easily. Depending on the weather, a skunk may nap for 2 weeks or for 3 months.

Raccoons

Raccoons have thick fur that is a mixture of gray, black, and brown. They have bushy tails with rings of black and gray. They have what looks like a black mask across the face and eyes. Raccoons will eat acorns, fruit, fish, frogs, earthworms, insect larvae, mice, and even raid food from garbage cans.

In warm areas, raccoons remain active all year. During winters that are very cold, raccoons will sleep for extended periods of time. They are very light sleepers, so many scientists do not consider raccoons to be true hibernators. A raccoon's pulse, breathing, and temperature drop only slightly when it sleeps. On a particularly warm winter day it may wander outside its den.

Raccoons prepare for hibernation by eating heavily in late summer and early fall. A 16-pound raccoon may eat 3 or 5 pounds of food a day. Raccoons head for their dens in October. Raccoons mate in winter around the end of January. Their young are born in spring and weigh only 2 ounces (60 grams). The young have fur at birth. The mothers nurse their kits and protect them until the following spring when they go out on their own.

Raccoons are light sleepers and may wake up and emerge from their dens on warmer winter days.

Even the smallest creatures, like this land snail, disappear during the winter months. They find places to hibernate in leaf litter, and under logs and stones.

Chapter Four

Under Dirt, Leaves, Logs, and Stones

It may be almost impossible to see the many small creatures that spend the winter in hiding against the cold winter backdrop. But they are everywhere under dirt, in leaf litter, in rotting logs, burrowed down into the mud, and beneath bark and stones. Harvester ants that scurried about in plain sight during the fall collecting grass and weed seeds have disappeared. As the snow falls, they live on their stored food, safe in their underground nest, behind a sealed entrance.

The bald-faced hornet queen has crawled under a rotting log to hibernate. The large Japanese hornets are hanging upside down from the ceilings of the chambers they have built in a nest they attached to a tree trunk. Those that survive become queens of new colonies in the spring. These and many other small animals spend the winter out of sight.

Snakes

Rattlesnakes are a type of pit **viper**. Their young are born in August or September and are immediately on their own. They are **carnivorous** and hunt food by scent, sound, and warmth. Often rattlesnakes lie in wait for prey to come within striking distance.

While the newborns are still quite young, it is time for snakes to begin their hibernation. They do not dig their own dens but use the holes or burrowing systems of other animals, preferring sunny hillsides and rocky outcrops.

Rattlesnakes curl up together to hibernate.

They **congregate** in the same places each year and coil up to hibernate with hundreds of other rattlesnakes until warm weather returns.

The red-sided garter snake lives as far north as Canada. In order to survive, this snake hibernates for almost nine months of the year. In summer, these snakes feed on worms, mice, and frogs. The females give birth to up to thirty young. By September, the snakes have crawled back deep underground. There they coil up with thousands of other snakes and await the coming of spring.

Ladybugs

Ladybird beetles, or ladybugs, hibernate. Some cluster around windows of homes where it is just the right temperature for them to hibernate. Others crawl under a log or into spaces in tree bark. Often several thousand collect in one spot. Some are found and eaten by hungry winter birds.

But birds are not the only ones to search for hibernating ladybugs. Ladybugs are popular because they eat

Ladybugs find a place to hibernate in the spaces of tree bark.

Mourning Cloak Butterflies

Mourning Cloak butterflies are found throughout eastern and western United States and southern Canada. The caterpillar feeds on roses and on elm, willow, and poplar trees. This large butterfly has a dark brown body and brown wings. The wings are yellow or white at the edges and have distinctive blue spots. The Mourning Cloak is one of the few butterflies that hibernates as an adult. This butterfly hibernates inside tree bark. It may sometimes be seen on a sunny day in very early spring flying over the snow.

hordes of harmful insects. Fruit growers and farmers in some parts of the country go into the mountains looking for ladybugs. They collect them by the thousands and keep them in cold storage until spring when they release them on farms and in orchards to eat pests.

After ladybugs mate in spring, the females deposit their eggs. Larvae hatch from the eggs in about a week, and in less than a month they become **pupae**. The pupal period lasts 1 week. Adults emerge and begin feeding on **aphids**. One ladybug will eat fifty or sixty aphids a day. As fall approaches, the ladybugs eat pollen that supplies the fat they need for their winter hibernation.

Snails and Slugs

There are many species of snails and slugs in North America. These **mollusks** are more closely related to octopuses than to insects. An interesting feature of both snails and slugs is their **slime**. To move, snails and slugs lay down a trail of slime and slide along it. Slugs can actually crawl unhurt over a razor blade by sliding over their silvery slime trail. When attacked by ants, they will bubble up slime in defense.

Snails and slugs prefer dark places during the day and feed at night. When it is warm, they crawl down into damp hiding places and absorb water through their skin. When snails hibernate, they seek out moist places and crawl into the topsoil or under a log or stones. They close up their shells with a cement-like material that they are able to produce in their bodies. Slugs have no external shells, but when they hibernate they cover themselves with a slimy material that helps keep them from drying out while they sleep underground.

A cluster of little brown bats hangs upside down in a cave during hibernation.

Chapter Five

In Caves and Crevices

Deep within a dark, damp cave are vertical shafts that trap the cold air. Its ceiling is a remarkable sight. Thousands of little brown bats huddle there, upside down, barely breathing, hanging from little hooks at the end of their wing joints. This spot is called a **hibernaculum**, and the bats hanging here are hibernating.

Caves are very different from one another. These differences are important in determining if a cave is a suitable spot for bat hibernation. It is estimated that fewer than 5 percent of the over 40,000 known caves in the United States can support bats. Such caves must have exactly the right temperature and **humidity** to meet the bats' needs. Since these caves are so scarce, some hibernating bats prefer abandoned mines.

Kinds of Bats

More than half of the bat species in North America use caves at least part of the year. Some bats, like the Red bat and Hoary bat, use caves in summer but then migrate to warmer areas when cold weather arrives. Many bats hibernate in winter. The little brown bat is the most common hibernating bat in North America.

A little brown bat has brownish, silky fur and is about 3 inches (8 cm) long. Although it can easily fit into the palm of your hand and weighs little more than a ball of cotton, its wingspread may be 10 inches (25 cm) wide. In the spring, a little brown bat weighs only 0.25 ounces (7.1 g). It eats its own weight in insects daily by using incredibly sharp pointy teeth that can crunch up an insect's tough outer skeleton. By the time it is ready to hibernate, the little brown bat weighs three times what it did in the spring and has put on layers of fat. This fat will be its energy source while the bat hibernates.

Come One, Come All

Many species of bat may use the same hibernation cave. In one roost in Europe, 25,000 bats of twelve different species were found.

Little brown bats have brownish, silky fur.

When the temperature begins to fall, many little brown bats fly to their winter hibernaculum. A bat wraps its wings like a blanket around itself before it begins hibernation. Typical hibernacula are damp places such as caves, abandoned mines, storm sewers, and cellars where there is high humidity and a stable temperature above freezing. Bats return to the same places year after year. In their resting state, the bats' bodies take on the same temperature as the air around them.

When a little brown bat hibernates, it breathes about once every minute. Awake, a little brown bat's heart beats over 400 times a minute, but during hibernation, it beats less than 25 times a minute. Little brown bats may wake during the winter. If there are insects or spiders in the cave, they may eat. If there is water, they drink, but they quickly return to hang upside down and sleep. Little brown bats hibernate for 3 or 4 months. Little brown bats awake from hibernation quickly in the spring, leave the cave, and fly in search of insects.

Females have their young in nursery colonies without the males. When the baby is born, the mother holds the little brown bat with her wings and nurses it. When the mother bat flies out to eat, she carries her baby with her. It holds on to its

Gray bats hang upside down in their hibernaculum.

mother's fur with teeth and claws. When it is between 2 weeks and 1 month old, a baby brown bat is ready to fly on its own.

Gray bats also hibernate. When they begin their long sleep, about 35 percent of their weight is fat. This fat is gone by spring. They wake every 12 to 30 days during hibernation to drink and to rid their bodies of waste products. If they are aroused too often during hibernation, they use up their stored fat reserves and may starve.

Although many people are afraid of bats and believe all sorts of superstitions about them, most bats are quite useful. They are particularly helpful in keeping down the insect population that damages crops. They are also important to pollination and seed dispersal.

Poorwill

Few people believed the story often told among Hopi Indians that some birds hibernate. The common belief was that when it got cold, birds migrated to warmer areas. Then a scientist verified the Hopi story in 1946. Dr. Edmund Jaeger and his

students found a hibernating poorwill in California's Chuckawalla Mountains.

Nuttal's poorwill, a gray and white cousin of the whip-poorwill, was sleeping in a hollow of the canyon wall. At first it was believed dead because no heartbeat was detected. Like other hibernators, the poorwill's temperature drops and its heartbeat slows. Finally detecting a faint heartbeat, the scientist banded the bird's leg. Future visits to the area proved that the poorwill returned to the same place each year to hibernate.

The poorwill's coloring helps it to blend in with its surroundings.

Crayfish hibernate by burying themselves in mud at the bottom of a pond.

Chapter Six

In the Mud

Some animals spend the winter hibernating in the mud. A crayfish, for example, buries itself in mud at the bottom of the pond. The surface of the pond may freeze, but the water at the bottom is not as cold. To survive in such conditions, these animals must be able to take in trapped oxygen through their skin.

Frogs

To prepare for winter, frogs, toads, and salamanders eat large amounts of food in the summer and fall, putting on extra fat. When the air temperature dips down toward freezing, these cold-blooded

When frogs are buried in mud hibernating, they take oxygen in through their skin instead of their lungs.

animals hibernate under leaves, logs, and rocks. And some frogs burrow in the muddy bottoms of ponds. The mud, which has air trapped in it, protects them from the colder water temperature. When they are hibernating, frogs take in oxygen through the skin instead of through their lungs.

In spring, male frogs dig out of the mud, croak to attract a mate, and begin their yearly cycle again. Spring peepers and wood frogs emerge from hibernation a month or two ahead of bullfrogs.

The most wide-ranging amphibian in North America is the leopard frog. The leopard frog has smooth green skin and white-edged dark blotches on its back. During the winter, this frog hibernates in the mud at the bottom of ponds or sometimes under submerged logs or rocks.

Turtles

A number of different turtles also bury themselves in mud for warmth in winter. Snapping turtles mate in spring. In summer, females lay their eggs on land in a shallow nest. The female covers the eggs with earth to keep them warm. The eggs hatch in 80 to 90 days, and the young snappers return to water. They begin eating and building up the supply of fat that they need to survive before winter comes and they must go into hibernation. When they hibernate, snapping turtles bury themselves in mud at the bottom of ponds, streams, or lakes.

The diamondback terrapin is a North American turtle that lives in salt marshes and nearby tidal waters. There are seven kinds, all found along the Atlantic and Gulf coasts from Massachusetts to Mexico.

Terrapins eat snails, crabs, shrimp, roots, and shoots. They have webbed feet and sharp claws. Their top shell is light brown, gray, or black and has lines shaped like diamonds.

Turtle Soup

The diamondback terrapin was hunted to near extinction to make terrapin soup in the late 1800s and early 1900s.

Snapping turtles bury themselves in mud to stay warm in the winter.

Alligators

Many alligators sleep in muddy dens. Adult alligators often create "gator holes" using their mouth and claws to uproot vegetation and clear a space. Then, by slashing with their tails, they wallow out a depression that holds water after the rains stop. Sometimes an alligator expands its gator hole by digging beneath an overhanging bank to create a den. It may tunnel as much as 20 feet into the bank. At the end of the tunnel it enlarges a chamber with a ceiling above the water line. To avoid summer's heat and winter's cold, an alligator may retreat to this muddy den.

When they hibernate, terrapins bury themselves in mud banks and their body functions slow. The terrapin doesn't come up to breathe during its hibernation period. It takes in oxygen from the water using a special membrane.

Fish

The blood of some Arctic and Antarctic fish may actually be a degree below freezing, but the fish and the water do not freeze. These fish live at the bottom of deep inlets, where the still, pure water is in a supercooled state. Ice crystals cannot easily form in this water.

Most freshwater fish remain active all winter. Some fish, such as carp and bass, become sluggish and probably do not eat. One kind of fish found in the United States hibernates. It is a type of pupfish or pond fish.

This slender fish has a short head and a broad mouth that is about 2 inches (5.1 cm) long. In winter, the pond fish wig-

gles down into the mud and hibernates. These fish are endangered and have become extinct in some places. One type of pond fish, the Pahrump killifish, is still found in three spots in Nevada: Corn Creek, Spring Mountain Ranch State Park, and the Shoshone Ponds Refugium.

Pahrump killifish bury themselves in mud at the bottom of a pond to hibernate.

This man examines a black bear as it hibernates.

Chapter Seven

Future Promise

Scientists still have much to learn about hibernation. To learn more, they try to study animals that hibernate. Scientists have taken small samples of blood from hibernating animals. They found that the blood has a substance in it, which they call HIT (Hibernation Inducement Trigger), that seems to cause hibernation to begin.

Scientists injected the blood taken from a hibernating squirrel into a different squirrel in the spring. They were able

Scientists were able to get a squirrel to hibernate in the spring by injecting it with the blood taken from a squirrel during hibernation.

to cause the squirrel to begin to hibernate even though it was the wrong time of year. But scientists still do not know much about how HIT works.

A number of doctors and psychiatrists have studied people who seem to become depressed in winter. They found that as the days grow shorter and the temperature drops, some people may respond by gaining weight and slowing down mentally and physically. This is similar to the response of animals getting ready to hibernate.

Just as animals respond in varying ways to winter, humans also adapt. Residents in extreme northern latitudes may use sun lamps to make up for the lack of natural sunlight, may modify their diet by eating heavier and richer foods, and will certainly dress appropriately in warm layers for the cold. Other people, who can afford it, copy the behavior of migrating animals. They take a mid-winter vacation to leave cold areas and visit the tropics!

Hibernation is of special interest to those people involved in the space program. Will it ever be possible for humans to hibernate using some chemical like HIT? If so, would lowering the bodily functions of humans and reducing their need for food, make it possible to go into deep space? Such fascinating possibilities encourage us to learn more about the process of hibernation.

Studying hibernation and its relationship to humans could help to improve how astronauts travel in space.

Glossary

adapt—to adjust or modify to meet new conditions

amphibians—a group of vertebrate animals that includes frogs, toads, newts, and salamanders

aphids—small insects with soft bodies that eat plant sap

carnivorous—eating the flesh of animals

cold-blooded—having a body temperature that adjusts to match the temperature of the surrounding area

congregate—to collect or assemble in a group

frost line—the depth at which soil no longer freezes

hibernaculum—a place such as a cave where bats spend the winter in a torpid state

hibernation—passing the winter in a dormant state

humidity—moisture or dampness

litter—a group of animal young

mammals—animals that nourish their young with milk

metabolism—the chemical changes in living cells that provide energy for life processes

migrating—moving from one region to another

mollusk—a group of invertebrates with soft bodies that are in most cases protected with a shell

pupae—insects at the stage between a larva and adult form when they transform while enclosed in a protective covering or cocoon

slime—the mucous secretion of slugs and snails

torpid—very sleepy and barely able to move

torpor—suspended animation or dormancy

viper—any of a group of venomous snakes

To Find Out More

Books

Bancroft, Henrietta and Richard G. Van Gelder. *Animals in Winter*. New York: HarperCollins, 1997.

Bennett, Paul. *Hibernation*. New York: Thomson Learning, 1995.

Berger, Melvin and Gilda Berger. *What Do Animals Do in Winter?: How Do Animals Survive the Cold*. Nashville, TN: Ideals Children's Books, 1995.

Facklam, Margery. *Do Not Disturb: The Mysteries of Animal Hibernation and Sleep*. San Francisco, CA: Sierra Club Books, 1989.

Kalman, Bobbie. *Why Do Animals Do That?* New York: Crabtree Publishing Co., 1997.

Stidworthy, John. *Hibernation*. New York: Gloucester Press, 1991.

Organizations and Online Sites

The Bear Den
http://www.nature-net.com/bears/
Contains information on behavior, reproduction, and hibernation of bears. Students have e-mail address to which they can send questions.

Carlsbad Caverns National Park
3225 National Parks Highway
Carlsbad, NM 88220
http://www.nps.gov/cave/
Describes the services available, including information on viewing bats, in Carlsbad Caverns.

Chicago's Lincoln Park Zoo
http://www.lpzoo.com
Learn about the animals at the Lincoln Park Zoo and search for information on other animals.

Jewel Cave National Monument
National Park Service
RR 1, Box 60AA
Custer, SD 57730
http://www.nps.gov/jeca/
Describes the hibernaculum for several species of bat in this third longest cave in the world.

A Note on Sources

In any kind of research, it is important to use as many resources as possible. Making use of the local library, I read all the books and articles on my topic that I can find. Then I consult with reference librarians and draw upon their expertise to lead me to other materials and make full use of interlibrary loan to secure books not in the local collection.

Books such as *Life in the Cold: Ecological, Physiological, and Molecular Mechanisms* (Cynthia Carey, Gregory L. Florant, Bruce A. Wunder, and Barbara Horwitz, eds., Westview Press, Boulder, CO, 1993) contained articles written by many scientists from papers presented at a series of international gatherings dedicated to understanding how animals survive cold conditions.

Print materials are not my only sources. I also go online and read as much information as I can find on the subject I am writing about. I talk with and interview people with specialized information on my topic.

The most difficult research aspect of this book was finding information about fish that hibernate. Relatively little has been written on this topic. In an oral interview, Professor Andrew Martin of the Biology Department of the University of Colorado, Boulder, supplied me with information about the rare pupfish and metabolic depression.

—*Phyllis J. Perry*

Index

Numbers in *italics* indicate illustrations.

About the Author

Phyllis J. Perry has published over 40 books for teachers and young people. Her newest book from Fulcrum Resources, *Keeping the Traditions: A Multicultural Resource*, documents the contributions to the United States of emigrants from twenty countries of the world. Books from Franklin Watts include: *The Snow Cats*, *Bats: The Amazing Upside-Downers*, *Crafty Canines: Coyotes, Foxes, and Wolves*, and *Freshwater Giants*. She did her undergraduate work at the University of California, Berkeley and received her doctorate in Curriculum and Instruction from the University of Colorado. Dr. Perry lives with her husband, David, in Boulder, Colorado where they enjoy the wildflowers, birds, and animals of the Rocky Mountains.